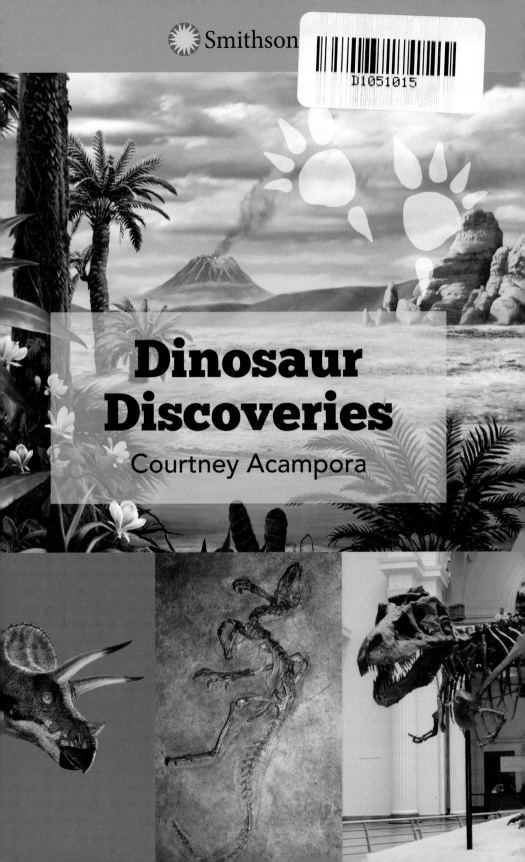

Smithson

Dinosaur Discoveries

Courtney Acampora

Contents

The World of Dinosaurs

Millions of years ago, hundreds of different types of **dinosaurs** lived on Earth.

Dinosaurs were prehistoric creatures that varied in size and color.

Avimimus

Amargasaurus

Dinosaur means "fearfully great lizard."

The Eras of Dinosaurs

Dinosaurs lived during the Mesozoic era. The Mesozoic era lasted one hundred and eighty-four million years.

The Mesozoic era is split into three periods.

The three periods are the Triassic, Jurassic, and Cretaceous.

Maiasaura

Dinosaurs lived for one hundred and sixty-five million years.

Dinosaurs became **extinct** sixty-six million years ago.

Psittacosaurus

Camarasaurus

Triassic Dinosaurs

Dinosaurs emerged near the end of the Triassic period.

Gorgosaurus

Iguanodon

Therizinosaurus

Triassic	Today

Earth looked much different during the Triassic period.

All of the continents were connected.

This large landmass was called **Pangaea**.

Triassic Dinosaurs

Eoraptor

Eoraptor was a Triassic dinosaur.

It was small and speedy, and lived in what is now Argentina.

Its name means "dawn stealer."

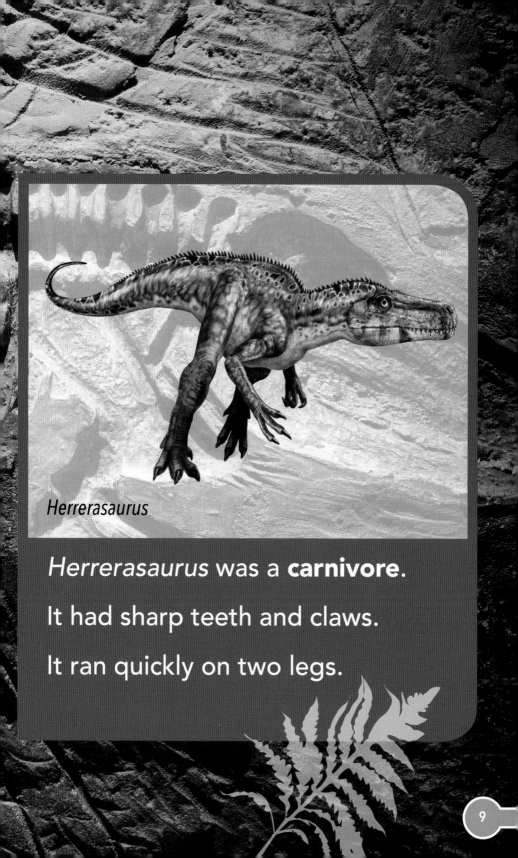

Herrerasaurus

Herrerasaurus was a **carnivore**.

It had sharp teeth and claws.

It ran quickly on two legs.

Diplodocus

Diplodocus was a giant dinosaur that was an **herbivore**.

Its long neck helped it reach leaves high up in trees.

Diplodocus lived in what is now the western United States.

Brachiosaurus

Brachiosaurus was an herbivore, too.

It ate four hundred pounds of plants a day!

Brachiosaurus means "arm lizard" because its front legs were longer than its back legs.

Stegosaurus

Stegosaurus had tough skin and a heavy, spiked tail.

Its back was covered in plates made from bone.

The plates helped protect *Stegosaurus's* body.

Allosaurus

Allosaurus's name means "different lizard," because its bones looked different from other dinosaurs bones.

Allosaurus's sharp teeth sliced through its **prey**.

Cretaceous Dinosaurs

Velociraptor

Velociraptor was a fierce, speedy dinosaur.

It had needle-sharp teeth and sharp claws.

It was an aggressive hunter, but was only the size of a large turkey!

Ankylosaurus

Ankylosaurus was as big as a small truck.

It was covered in hard, bony plates that protected it from **predators**.

Its tail had a bony knob that it swung like a club.

Cretaceous Dinosaurs

Triceratops

Triceratops means "three-horned face" because it had three sharp horns on its head.

It had a big frill on its neck.

Triceratops had a sharp beak used to crush through tough plants.

Tyrannosaurus rex

Tyrannosaurus rex was a fierce hunter with lots of sharp teeth and a powerful bite.

Its arms were unusually small and short, but were surprisingly strong.

Tyrannosaurus rex may have been covered in feathers!

Dinosaur Extinction

Dinosaurs roamed Earth for 165 million years.

They became extinct at the end of the Cretaceous period.

Scientists believe an asteroid smashed into Earth.

This may have cooled the planet and caused their extinction.

Did you know?

A large crater in Mexico is believed to be the site of the asteroid crash.

Fossils

Everything we know about dinosaurs comes from their **fossils** and descendants, birds.

Fossils are the remains of animals preserved in the earth.

Dinosaur fossils formed because their bodies were covered by mud, sand, or other earth in a watery environment.

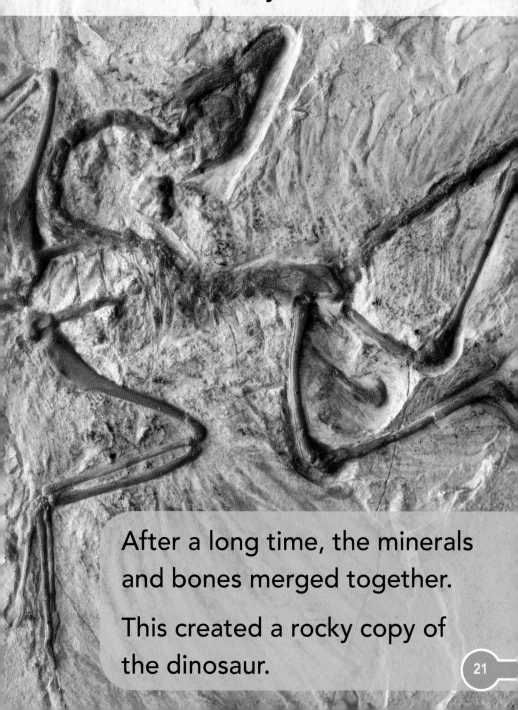

After a long time, the minerals and bones merged together.

This created a rocky copy of the dinosaur.

Fossils

Paleontologists study dinosaur fossils.

Sometimes everyday people, or kids, find fossils too!

Paleontologists find fossils of bones, teeth, and even footprints.

Fossils of teeth determine if a dinosaur was a meat eater or plant eater.

Fossilized footprints show how dinosaurs moved.

Fossilized eggs have also been discovered.

Amazing Discoveries

Sir Richard Owen was a British paleontologist.

He gave dinosaurs their name in 1842.

He studied fossils in England and concluded that they were from a group he called dinosaurs.

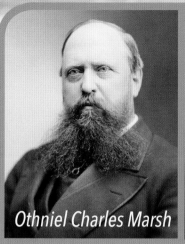

Othniel Charles Marsh

Edward Drinker Cope

The Dinosaur Wars

Othniel Charles Marsh and Edward Drinker Cope were paleontologists.

In the 1800s they searched for fossils in the American West.

They were competitive and tried to find more fossils than each other.

Marsh and Cope discovered over one hundred new dinosaur species.

Amazing Discoveries

Roy Chapman Andrews went on an expedition to the Gobi Desert in the 1920s.

The Gobi Desert is in Asia.

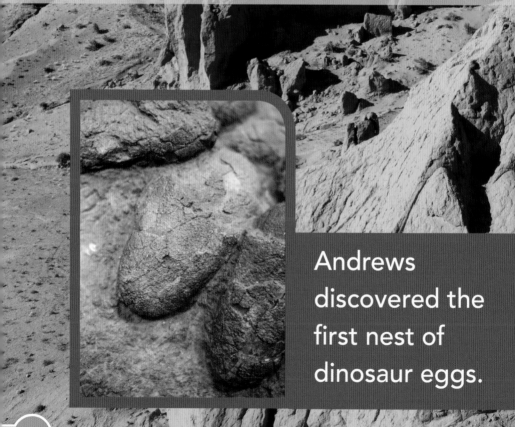

Andrews discovered the first nest of dinosaur eggs.

Sue the *T. rex*

In 1990, the best-preserved *T. rex* fossil was discovered in South Dakota.

It was discovered by paleontologist Sue Hendrickson.

The *T. rex* was named Sue after her!

Uncovering Dinosaurs

Spinosaurus

Dinosaurs dominated Earth for millions of years.

Amazing dinosaur discoveries have been made from the fossils they left behind.

Corythosaurus

Euoplocephalus tutus

Paleontologists are continually finding dinosaur fossils.

These discoveries reveal more and more about dinosaurs.

There is still so much more to uncover about dinosaurs!

Dinosaur Discoveries QUIZ

1. What are the three periods that made up the Mesozoic era?
   a) Miocene, Pliocene, Pleistocene
   b) Triassic, Jurassic, and Cretaceous
   c) Pleistocene, Holocene, Quaternary

2. What was the large landmass made up of all the continents called?
   a) Pangaea
   b) Gobi
   c) North America

3. What do scientists think caused the dinosaurs extinction?
   a) Tsunami
   b) Asteroid
   c) Earthquake

4. What do paleontologists do?
    a) Study dinosaur fossils
    b) Map Pangaea
    c) Study asteroids

5. Who gave dinosaurs their name?
    a) Roy Chapman Andrews
    b) Edward Drinker Cope
    c) Sir Richard Owens

6. Which of these can be fossils?
    a) Dinosaur eggs
    b) Footprints
    c) All of the above

Answers: 1.b 2.a 3.b 4.a 5.c 6.c

GLOSSARY

carnivore: an animal that eats meat

dinosaur: main group of archosaur reptiles that lived during the Mesozoic era. Includes modern birds

extinct: no longer living

fossil: the remains of prehistoric life found in stone

herbivore: an animal that eats plants

paleontologist: scientist who studies fossils

Pangaea: a supercontinent made up of all the landmasses on Earth

predator: an animal that hunts other animals for food

prey: an animal hunted by other animals for food